NO
BULLSH!T
Marketing

NO
BULLSH!T
Marketing

17 CONTRARIAN WAYS
TO INCREASE REFERRALS FOR
HEALTHCARE SERVICES

DAVE MASTOVICH

INDIE BOOKS
INTERNATIONAL

ISBN-13: 978-1-957651-84-2
Library of Congress Control Number: 2024916417

Designed by theBookDesigners

INDIE BOOKS
INTERNATIONAL

INDIE BOOKS INTERNATIONAL®, INC.
2511 WOODLANDS WAY
OCEANSIDE, CA 92054
www.indiebooksintl.com

Contents

1

WHY SYSTEMATIC REFERRAL SOURCE
MARKETING IS YOUR UNTAPPED ADVANTAGE

Success in healthcare springs from exceptional patient care. But there's another dimension nearly as crucial—referral source marketing.

In the interconnected world of healthcare, professionals rely on each others' expertise to guide patient care. It's not about business transactions. It's about ensuring that patients, members, and residents receive the best possible care by connecting with the right specialists and services.

The healthcare landscape is a network of trust where professionals lean on one another to extend the continuum of care. It's a realm where the quality of patient care and the growth of healthcare services are intrinsically linked.

Whether you're a physical therapist aiming to broaden your client base, a durable medical equipment provider seeking more physician referrals, the leader of a multi-physician group striving to boost patient volume, or a senior living executive working to attract more residents, this book is for you. It's also for any healthcare professional seeking the tools and strategies necessary to drive substantial, sustainable growth.

It's not enough to simply increase referrals sporadically when you notice a dip in volume. The real breakthrough comes from systematic referral source marketing, which is about reaching, connecting, and engaging with current and prospective referral sources—something that's not yet common practice. This insight dawned on me early in my career while I worked for multiple media companies as a teenager. Now, I'm ready to pass on the practical strategies and tactics I've learned along the way to drive growth for your healthcare organization.

HOW RADIO LED TO A HEALTHCARE MARKETING DISCOVERY

This rebirth story takes two radio stations from the outhouse to the penthouse. And it led me to an important discovery for healthcare services.

It's the early '90s and the place is Johnstown, Pennsylvania, ninety miles east of Pittsburgh. This is one of the top one hundred radio markets in America, yet two stations I worked at as a teenager had gone bankrupt, and the owners needed someone to lead a turnaround. Days after graduating college, full of confidence and not completely understanding what the situation would require, I said, "I'll take this on."

The two stations—an AM station that tried to be everything to everybody and an FM station that tried to be everything to everybody—were ranked at the bottom of fourteen stations in the market. Armed with the knack of engaging diverse party crowds from time as a DJ and with my marketing professor's lessons on market segmentation, I championed a new strategy. We sharply defined the target audience for each station to transform them from jack-of-all-trades to masters of their respective niches. This pivot was key to cultivating a dedicated listener base and propelling the stations from rock bottom to market leaders.

The AM station went to twenty-four-hour news, sports, and talk. It wasn't for everybody, but one group was intensely interested in this station.

The FM station was a bigger challenge. At first, we made it a hit station, all hits, but this was still too broad. Then we zeroed in on making it a country station, WMTN, the Mountain. The market adopted it, and the station was successful, becoming number one.

The AM station was number three in the market, so we had two of the top three stations.

Understanding that this could be applied to other industries, my attention turned to healthcare services. If leveraging market segmentation and telling a story that mattered to the target markets could boost two radio stations, it could do the same for healthcare services.

CROSS-POLLINATING FROM RADIO TO HEALTHCARE SERVICES

Many great ideas in business are not new ideas. They are just ideas borrowed from somewhere else.

After leaving the radio stations and beginning to work in healthcare, an opportunity arose to build an occupational health program to reach local company leaders and their employees. This program attempted to prevent workplace injuries and strived to get injured people healthy and back to regular living as quickly as possible. It was important to apply what I learned from one industry to another.

When we built that occupational healthcare program, we had to talk to businesses and learn how to get them to sign up for the service. We found that clients would refer us to others once we built a strong relationship and proved value. It made sense to apply the same approach for other healthcare services when those providers needed more patients. I realized that referral source marketing was a key component of a strategic, comprehensive growth marketing plan for healthcare providers.

Changes in healthcare reimbursement at that time meant that the old way of doing business—relying primarily on treating as many patients in the hospital as possible to generate revenue—would no longer be financially viable. My next turnaround challenge required us to focus more of our efforts on our offerings outside of the hospital through services like home health, outpatient physical therapy, same-day surgery, and hospice care.

Our strategy involved examining who was currently referring patients to the outpatient service providers, who could have been referring more, and who wasn't referring at all but should have been. Then, we tailored outreach marketing to referral sources, which led to growth in patient volumes for each of these healthcare service areas.

We also developed many primary care centers throughout the region and needed to recruit physicians and grow their practices. Again, the secret in each of those instances was referral source marketing.

2

THE SIX TARGET MARKETS THAT REALLY MATTER

There is an adage that says, "If an arrow does not hit a target, it is never the fault of the target."

There is a targeting magic in tapping into the power of referrals from physicians, surgeons, hospital case managers, and social service agencies for clients across the healthcare space.

If you are in the healthcare services sector, you know your business differs from other products and services.

The healthcare services sector needs to understand six target markets, especially the referral piece.

This market can include anything in the healthcare sector, ranging from physical therapy, rehab, senior living, assisted living, independent living, home healthcare, hospice, home medical equipment, Medicare Advantage programs, hospitals, physician practices, and even periodontists.

HEALTHCARE SERVICES IS A DIFFERENT KIND OF BEAST

Leaders from the whole spectrum of healthcare services will benefit from understanding why these six target markets matter and by building a comprehensive growth marketing strategy to drive more referrals, patients, members, and residents.

Alas, poor marketing. Of all the business disciplines, marketing is probably the least understood.

Perhaps the misunderstanding occurs because most business leaders are more familiar with the other disciplines than they are with marketing. When you think about it, anybody who's running a company or in a leadership role has to have some degree of financial and business management understanding:

- *The financial aspect* must be understood to start and run a successful business.

- *The organizational development part* must be understood to hire, lead, and manage people.

- *Operations* facilitate bringing the overall business into a leadership position and many leaders either have experience in operations or a base level understanding of it.

As a result, most people have worked through some of those business disciplines but really haven't "done" marketing even when they think they have.

That's where the problem lies because most business leaders don't fully understand marketing and the target markets they need to reach. They end up neglecting one, two, or three of the six target markets that matter.

MEET THE CRUCIAL SIX TARGET MARKETS

In the healthcare services industry, understanding and effectively communicating with our target markets is vital for sustained growth and impact. Here are the six key target markets, each requiring a tailored approach:

- *Current customers:* This group includes patients in clinical settings, members in health plans, residents in care facilities, and others who are directly receiving our services. Communication here is focused on trust building, providing health education, and ensuring satisfaction to encourage retention and positive word-of-mouth.

- *Prospective or potential customers:* Potential customers are those seeking healthcare options. We must understand their needs and concerns to effectively position our services as their best choice, using targeted outreach to guide them toward choosing our services.

- *Current employees:* Our healthcare professionals and support staff are the backbone of service delivery. Engaging them involves internal communications that foster a supportive culture, ongoing education, and recognition of their hard work and dedication.

- *Potential employees:* With the competition for top talent in healthcare, attracting potential employees means showcasing an attractive culture, clear career progression, and the value of their work toward a greater mission in the community.

- *Current referral sources:* These are the partners who trust us enough to send patients our way, such as other physicians, healthcare organizations, social services, and case managers. Our communication with them needs to reaffirm our commitment to quality care and keep them informed on our latest services and successes.

- *Potential referral sources:* You need a systematic marketing approach with people who can refer to you. To engage potential referrers, we need to articulate our unique selling points and demonstrate our successful outcomes. It's about building new relationships on the foundation of credibility and mutual benefit.

But beware, there is a danger lurking that can kill your best referral efforts. Please pardon the candor, but that danger is called bullsh!t marketing. How to avoid it is covered in the next chapter.

3

YOUR HOW-TO GUIDE TO
AVOID BULLSH!T MARKETING

What is bullsh!t marketing?

It's easier to first explain what no bullsh!t marketing is and how I came to live that mantra.

Let me introduce you to my anti-bullsh!t marketing mentor. One of the coolest things in my early college career was my exposure to Philip Kotler.

Most people in marketing might not even know who Kotler is, and even fewer know he is considered the father of modern marketing. Kotler taught me theories about consumer behavior, market segmentation, and the four *P*'s of marketing.[1]

The four *P*'s are product, price, place, and promotion. Often referred to as a marketing mix, they provide a framework that companies can use to successfully market a product or service to consumers. Those concepts continue to be employed because they are as strong and relevant today as when they were first presented.

THE FOUR P'S MEET A PUNCH IN THE MOUTH

There's an important point about theories learned from books compared to what happens in real life, as I realized in my work with the radio stations. It's like an old line from former heavyweight boxing champ Mike Tyson, who said, "Everybody has a plan until you get punched in the mouth."[2]

You can prepare for challenges but then when you get punched in the mouth, how you react is what defines you. All of Kotler's teachings were great in my eyes. But then, when I figuratively (almost literally a few times) got punched in the mouth while driving change at those radio stations, I realized those theories would have to be adjusted, tweaked, and enhanced.

Each small and medium-sized business owner gave us insights about what was needed to turn things around. It was important for us to ask open-ended questions, then shut up and listen. Next, we took those insights back to our team and figured out ways to make the positive change a reality. The same thing happened during each of those healthcare turnarounds and growth opportunities.

NO BULLSH!T MARKETING OPPORTUNITY #1:
UNDERSTAND WHAT MARKETING IS

My definition of real marketing is finding out what your current and prospective customers want, developing it, giving it to them when and where they want it at a price they're willing to pay, and then telling them about it again and again.

The problem is that most marketing focuses on the last part, telling them about it again and again.

Telling current and potential customers about your products and services repeatedly is one piece of marketing. But first, understanding who needs to be reached and clearly defining those ideal, right-fit customers is the starting point. Finding out what they want by asking them and listening, then developing a plan or changing what you already have, is also part of marketing. So is giving your healthcare service to them when and where they want it at a price they're willing to pay. Once you've done all that, you do the fun part of repeatedly telling them your story.

Far too often, the focus is primarily on telling them about your services again and again. Instead, systematically gather insights by asking the right questions and actively listening. Define and drill down your target markets with actual data instead of gut instincts. Let behavioral science drive the creative art and commit to a comprehensive and strategic marketing approach.

NO BULLSH!T MARKETING OPPORTUNITY #2: LEVERAGE TWO SEPARATE YET EQUAL DISCIPLINES

Another piece of bullsh!t marketing is thinking that one specific tactic is marketing. For example, some people believe sales is marketing. It isn't, although sales are very important. Sales *can* drive the company, but your marketing strategy and activities *should* drive it. Sales are a tactical component, whereas marketing is strategic.

Most people focus too much on one area of marketing, such as digital marketing content, search engine optimization, paid advertising or other tactical marketing. They tend to become myopic and often don't realize that real marketing involves a strategic framework that ties the tactical components together

It all snowballs into a misperception among customers of marketing, whether internal leaders or external customers, because we, as marketers, aren't accurately portraying the totality of marketing. We aren't living the no bullsh!t definition of marketing tied to clearly defined target markets, then finding out what the customer wants, developing it, and giving it to them when and where they want it at a price they're willing to pay. You cannot get by with just a couple of stand-alone marketing tactics. You need a strategic growth marketing strategy.

NO BULLSH!T MARKETING OPPORTUNITY #3:
EARN AND COMMAND YOUR RESPECT AS A MARKETER

Not too long ago, marketing was a dirty word in healthcare.

Here's an example. I was recruited to drive growth at a struggling hospital that was the largest employer in their region. The new CEO and board weren't exactly sure about referral source marketing and the other key solutions I suggested while they tried to convince me to take the job. But they knew that marketing was needed to turn things around.

Like most turnaround situations, we quickly realized things were worse than we thought when we began digging into the data and systematically gathering insights. The new CEO leaned heavily on those insights, and we built a strategic growth marketing strategy to position the hospital differently and tell the real story to current and potential patients, employees, and referral sources.

The board chair insisted that even though I would be part of the senior leadership team and serve as a VP or chief marketing officer, my position title would be director of marketing.

The CEO basically said, "To hell with the title. You're going to drive this with me. We're making this happen."

That convinced me to take the job, after which a funny thing happened. When people referred to the senior leadership team, they would say, "The VPs and Dave meet every Thursday." So, there was this implication that there was the CEO, four VPs, and Dave. At first, it seemed an insult, but then I realized it was great for my reputation.

This story shows how weird people can get about marketing. Even today, many companies struggle to give marketing the proper respect and seat at the table with finance and operations. That's bullsh!t, and you, as a marketer, need to first earn that respect by defining marketing for them and showing them how it's both a science and an art. Behavioral science and quantifiable data drive the creative art of changing behaviors and mindsets.

Then, once you've done that, command and demand the respect that marketing professionals deserve. Discuss how strategic marketing key performance indicators (KPIs) can help senior leaders build and enhance the organization's strategies. Show how marketing can help with recruiting, retention, and team results. Outline how marketing drives lead generation and provides the stories to close the sale.

NO BULLSH!T MARKETING OPPORTUNITY #4: DON'T NEGLECT WHAT SHOULD BE OBVIOUS TARGET MARKETS

Sometimes, the obvious slips past us all. We miss the forest for the trees.

Companies are missing two target markets that might seem obvious but are neglected from a marketing standpoint.

Marketing within healthcare is rife with untapped potential, teetering on the edge of mediocrity due to two glaringly neglected areas. Ignoring these is a one-way ticket to becoming a bullsh!t marketer, lost in a sea of *coulda*'s and *shoulda*'s. Let's cut through that noise.

First, we dig into referral source marketing—the cornerstone of this no-nonsense approach. If you're in the healthcare game, regardless of your organization's size or niche, you need a strategy as precise as a surgeon's scalpel. This requires a systematic action method, not just a checklist to feel good about.

"Systematic" doesn't mean drowning in a deluge of data; that's self-sabotage with extra steps. Big healthcare behemoths often fall into this trap, obsessing over the quantity of data like it's a collector's item. But here's the kicker: data is cold and lifeless until you breathe meaning into it. You must mine it for insights, sculpting it into a treasure trove of actionable intel. Remember, striving for perfection is a fool's errand if it paralyzes you. It's like having a medical breakthrough but never starting the clinical trial.

On the flip side, smaller healthcare outfits have floundered from lacking even the basics of data tracking. Who's referring to whom, when, and why? That's your bread and butter. If you're in this boat, it's time to set sail. Start simple but start now. Gather. Track. Analyze. In the midst of this, never underestimate the gut instincts of your leaders. Marry instinct with insight, and you've got a power couple to put your referral source marketing on the map.

Ultimately, it's about striking that delicate balance—where data meets gut, systematic meets human.

Building on the momentum of referral source marketing,

we pivot to the second and equally crucial battlefield—our own corridors, the lifeblood of any healthcare organization—the employees. Enter business-to-employee (B2E) marketing, the unsung hero of internal dynamics. This isn't just some buzzword; it's a game changer that we've adopted, refined, and owned.

Consider this: your employees are your first line of ambassadors. They wield the power to make or break your brand with a single interaction, referral, or display of satisfaction or dissatisfaction.

The three *R*'s of B2E—recruiting, retention, and results—are the foundation of a flourishing healthcare ecosystem.

When it comes to talent acquisition, think of it as the courtship phase. You're not just looking for talent but attracting future brand ambassadors. This requires a narrative that resonates, one that goes beyond the paycheck and taps into purpose and passion. And once they're on board, retention becomes your focus. It consists of cultivating an environment so enriching that leaving is the last thing on their minds. This is where your internal communication strategies must shine, spotlighting achievements, fostering growth, and nurturing a culture that celebrates every team member.

But what about the results? This is where the rubber meets the road. Enhanced productivity stems from clarity, coherence, and a sense of belonging. Better internal communication is about ensuring every team member understands their role in the larger narrative. It's also about them seeing the effect of their work on their own growth and on the health and wellness of the people they serve.

NO BULLSH!T MARKETING OPPORTUNITY #5: TURN "BECAUSE THAT'S HOW WE'VE ALWAYS DONE IT" INTO GROWTH MARKETING

What does no bullsh!t marketing mean? It's tied to many core values. The first is to think differently and challenge assumptions. This means avoiding statements heard so many times, such as, "That's how we've always done it." And it's about deep thinking, which is one of the key elements of no bullsh!t marketing.

No bullsh!t marketing is also about driving positive change. It's not just about doing the same old, same old to make things look pretty or generate more contact form submissions. It is about adapting, innovating, and growing.

In the throes of healthcare transformation, the phrase "Because that's how we've always done it" is the antithesis of progress. It is a red flag that signals an opportunity for change.

Whenever I stepped into a leadership role at a healthcare organization teetering on the edge of demise, I instinctively asked, "Why?" at every turn. The responses often unveiled a tapestry of outdated practices, each thread woven with the same refrain: "Because that's how we've always done it." That was unacceptable. It was the sound of gears grinding to a halt, the sight of potential withering on the vine.

Challenging the status quo became my modus ope-
randi. Refusing to accept tradition as the blueprint for the
future, I asked, "How can we do this better?" and "What
does our customer really need?" These questions became
the catalyst for innovation. They led to the dismantling of
archaic systems and the birth of streamlined processes that
met and anticipated customer needs. This wasn't change
for the sake of change—it was strategic, necessary, and
growth marketing in action.

No bullsh!t marketing opportunity #5 is about having
the courage to dismantle the machinery of mediocrity and
replace it with something extraordinary. It consists of leveraging deep thinking to dissect every process, service, and
communication through the lens of value and effectiveness.

So, we cut through the noise and the nonsense. We
replaced the "we've always done it this way" with "we do it
this way because it works, is efficient, and puts our patients
first." This became our new mantra, reverberating through
the halls and transforming the culture from the inside out.

You, too, will drive positive change by embodying
adaptability, innovation, and growth principles. That's the
heartbeat of no bullsh!t marketing: relentless, bold, and
always questioning the status quo to drive personal, professional, and organizational growth.

NO BULLSH!T MARKETING OPPORTUNITY #6:
CREATIVE PROBLEM-SOLVING BUILDS TRUST,
CREATIVE SELLING USUALLY DOESN'T

No bullsh!t marketing opportunity #6 is all about the art of creative problem-solving. This principle is at the heart of authentic marketing and is deeply intertwined with our core values: think, adapt, innovate, grow, and communicate. These aren't just words; they are the gears of a well-oiled machine that drives toward success.

Creative problem-solving transcends the boundaries of traditional marketing. It's about delving deep into a challenge's essence and uncovering solutions that address the issue and elevate the customers' experience. It's about crafting solutions that resonate on a personal level and speak to the needs and desires of our audience. This is where real connection happens, which is the foundation of trust.

Trust is a fortress built over time, with consistency and reliability as its mortar. In no bullsh!t marketing, we aim to sell, strive, and serve. And in that service, we commit to transparency and integrity. When we communicate with our customers, it's not a monologue; it's a dialogue. It's not about over-hyping our products or services but about presenting them in a clear, straightforward, and memorable way.

In this ethos, there's an inherent vulnerability—an acknowledgment that we, too, are human. We may not have all the answers, but we are determined to find them.

This human element brings us closer to our team members and our audience. In moments of crisis, this vulnerability becomes our strength, allowing us to demonstrate sensitivity and empathy and to fortify meaningful relationships.

No bullsh!t marketing is a mindset, a commitment to eschew the smoke and mirrors in favor of a clear vision. It's a pledge to listen actively, to respond thoughtfully, and to engage genuinely. When the old marketing world zigs with deception and short-term gains, we zag with honesty and sustainable growth. That's the kind of creative problem-solving that builds trust.

NO BULLSH!T MARKETING OPPORTUNITY #7: LEVERAGE BOTH 80/20 ANALYSIS AND 80/20 THINKING

No bullsh!t marketing opportunity #7 is a clarion call to embrace the power of 80/20 thinking and 80/20 analysis—two facets of the same gem that can transform the landscape of any business, especially within the intricate systems of healthcare marketing.

Also known as the Pareto Principle, 80/20 thinking is a strategic framework that teaches us to identify the most impactful elements in any scenario. As Richard Koch describes in his book *The 80/20 Principle: The Secret to Achieving More with Less*, in any population, some things are likely to be much more important than others. A good benchmark or hypothesis is that 80 percent of results or outputs flow from 20 percent of causes and sometimes from a much smaller proportion of forces.

It's about focusing on the 20 percent of efforts yielding 80 percent of the results. It's a mindset that prioritizes effectiveness over busyness and effect over activity. When we apply 80/20 thinking, we're consciously investing our resources—time, energy, and capital—into the areas that will drive the most significant returns. It's about working smarter, not harder, and making every action count.

Meanwhile, 80/20 analysis involves dissecting your operations, marketing campaigns, and customer interactions to pinpoint the 20 percent driving your success. This analysis requires digging into data, understanding customer behaviors, and evaluating outcomes. It consists of leveraging analytics to inform our decisions, cutting through the clutter to reveal the high-yield activities.

When combined, 80/20 thinking and 80/20 analysis embody systems thinking—a holistic approach to innovation that considers the interrelatedness of all components. Systems thinking in no bullsh!t marketing demands that we look beyond the obvious, asking how each piece of the marketing puzzle influences the others and how they collectively contribute to the overarching goal.

Integrating 80/20 thinking into our strategic mindset allows us to steer clear of conventional wisdom that spreads efforts thinly across all fronts. Instead, we concentrate on the vital few: the customers who advocate for us, the marketing channels that bring the best return on investment

(ROI), and the messaging that resonates the most. Think of it as recognizing patterns of success and doubling down on them.

On the other hand, 80/20 analysis is about getting your hands dirty with the data, following the trail of numbers to unearth the golden insights. It's an unapologetic dive into what really works, bolstered by the confidence from evidence and results.

Leveraging both 80/20 analysis and 80/20 thinking is about cultivating a mindset and methodology that consistently seeks to optimize and streamline. It's the antithesis of "spray and pray" tactics. It's targeted, it's precise, and it's ruthlessly efficient. Ultimately, no bullsh!t marketing is a way to think, operate, and innovate. It's the art of eliminating excess to reveal the sleek, powerful core of true value that drives growth and success.

NO BULLSH!T MARKETING OPPORTUNITY #8: UNDERSTAND THAT GROWTH MEANS MORE THAN TOP-LINE GROWTH

No bullsh!t marketing opportunity #8 strikes at the heart of what it truly means to grow. In the most holistic sense, growth transcends the conventional fixation on top-line metrics. Sales are vital; they keep the lights on, fuel innovation, and enable expansion. But a deeper, more resonant kind of growth is often overshadowed—the development of people who are any organization's heartbeat.

Empathy stands at the forefront of this philosophy. It's not just about understanding your customer's needs; it's about feeling them. In no bullsh!t marketing, emotional quotient (EQ) trumps intelligence quotient (IQ) because business is, at its core, about human connections. EQ is the undercurrent that powers genuine relationships, drives customer loyalty, and creates a work environment that's more than a cog in a corporate machine—it's a thriving ecosystem of passionate individuals.

Professional growth is about expanding skill sets, pushing boundaries, and fostering an environment where continuous learning is the norm, not the exception. It means equipping your team with the tools and opportunities to excel—not just in their current roles but also in shaping their future paths.

And then there's personal growth, which involves encouraging your team to develop as employees and individuals. It's recognizing that when your team members grow personally—whether by pursuing passions, nurturing their well-being, or engaging in community service—they bring a richer, more nuanced perspective to their professional roles.

In no bullsh!t marketing, growth is a multifaceted endeavor. It's about aiming for that top-line growth while simultaneously nurturing the bottom line through efficiency and innovation. But it doesn't end there. It's also about fostering an environment where personal and professional growth are encouraged and seen as critical to the organization's success.

When we understand that growth is multidimensional, we unlock unprecedented potential. We create a culture that values and invests in its people, understanding that their development is linked to the organization's trajectory. This is the essence of no bullsh!t marketing—authentic, inclusive, and profound human growth. It consists of building a legacy beyond numbers, measured by the impact on people's lives, both within and outside the company.

My marketing opportunities were put to the test with a billion-dollar healthcare system, which is explored in the following chapter.

4

LESSONS FROM A BILLION-DOLLAR HEALTHCARE SYSTEM

The New York Yankees have a hundred-year track record of success in Major League Baseball.

Legend has it that the run of success was triggered in 1920 when Babe Ruth was sold by the Boston Red Sox to the Yankees for a hundred thousand dollars, which started the Yankee dynasty. In Boston, they called it the Curse of the Bambino.

Through the years, many successful players came to play for the Yankees and had their greatest success. Roger Maris went from the A's to the Yankees, set a home run record, and won the MVP two years in a row. Dave Winfield went from the Padres to the Yankees and had an incredibly successful run that landed him in the Hall of Fame. Roger Clemens went from Toronto to the Yankees and finally won a World Series. Reggie Jackson came to the Yankees and became known as Mr. October for his play in the postseason. As Frank Sinatra sang, "If I can make it there, I'll make it anywhere."[3]

"WHEN ARE YOU GOING TO COME PLAY FOR THE YANKEES?"

It has been a blessing to be a part of multiple turnarounds in my career, including the radio stations and three other healthcare-related ones. What was great about all the turnarounds was building a team—keeping and coaching up some existing team players, finding some new ones—and then seeing that team come together to drive growth. That changes things so much; it's exhilarating. It's something for each of those team members to be proud of because they not only helped thousands of employees but also helped so many communities to have the healthcare services they needed.

As growth and turnaround opportunities continued to be part of my career, I kept running into some of the major players from one of the most forward-thinking healthcare markets in the country. Pittsburgh is a medium-sized big city, but on the healthcare side, it has always "played big": the new medical approaches, the physicians, the surgeries, and some milestones and "firsts" in healthcare.

One of the top people, the number two person in a larger system being built, saw me and said, "When are you going to come play for the Yankees?"

And I asked, "Huh?"

And he jokingly said, "Well, you're out there fixing things with duct tape, chewing gum, and no money. You're helping these community hospitals and these medium-sized healthcare systems. When are you going to play for the Yankees?

We're building something here that's not just national. It's going to be international."

He was talking about something intriguing—the concept of an integrated financial healthcare delivery system. At that time, there was some experimentation on the West Coast, but not much beyond that. Each city or region across the U.S. had solo practicing physicians who each had power and ran their practice like a fiefdom. The local community hospitals also had an undue influence in their communities. The same was true with healthcare insurers.

Blue Cross Blue Shield was one insurance company that typically dominated, like in western Pennsylvania. They had such a brand name that people would tell us during our research, "I get my Blue Cross and Blue Shield from HealthAmerica." Well, that's when you know you have a brand name—the market thinks of you as the product. And so, there was a monopoly on the financial side.

What was intriguing was this leader's talk about an integrated financial healthcare delivery system. In it, you would bring each disparate element into a team, with the financial arm working with the physician arm, which was working with the hospital arm, which was working with the healthcare services provider arm, all working together.

That's the first thing that was compelling.

Then, this leader, who was with the University of Pittsburgh Medical Center (UPMC) said, "I also want to have a relationship with the Steelers and Penguins because I see sports as the fabric of our communities, and we can tell our story by partnering with them. I need you to drive that sports marketing."

Remember the 1996 movie *Jerry Maguire*, written and directed by Cameron Crowe? Tom Cruise stars as maverick sports agent Jerry Maguire, who marries his assistant Dorothy, played by Renée Zellweger. Jerry's marriage with Dorothy deteriorates as she notices he seems to care more about clients than her, so they separate. In an iconic movie scene, Jerry returns home months later to beg Dorothy for a second chance, making an impassioned speech in front of a living room full of guests that he wants her back. She stops him by saying: "Shut up. Just shut up. You had me at hello."[4]

That applied to me because I almost said to him, "Shut up, you had me at hello."

When I came to UPMC, the system had just under $1 billion in revenue, which is a lot. However, it grew even bigger, to more than $10 billion in annual revenue in a short time. The UPMC approach, focusing on growth marketing, was ahead of the curve, turning the healthcare system into something special.

A marketing laboratory was created for growth marketing, brand storytelling, market segmentation, and testing my healthcare referral maximizer, which was used continually to drive people to refer to all our healthcare service providers, whether physical therapy, home health, assisted living, etc.

And so, UPMC became a laboratory for ideas, with a number of talented people who were turned loose to maximize our unique abilities. That's where my ideas and creative solutions began to crystalize because we had a budget and an opportunity to reach and influence people. We were trying to create a better healthcare experience by expanding and improving the care. It was a wonderful time for me when a marketing laboratory provided all the tools needed to drive massive growth.

MEET THE HEALTHCARE REFERRAL MAXIMIZER

The healthcare referral maximizer is a strategic system designed to optimize the way you reach, connect with, and engage your referral sources. It starts with a systematic approach to gathering insights, which involves a deep dive into referral data across multiple years. This analysis isn't just about numbers—it's about understanding the story behind your referrals: identifying who they come from, discerning patterns over time, and recognizing the most fruitful sources.

This system is underpinned by what I call the Pareto Principle Plus. It goes beyond the basic 80/20 analysis— where a majority of referrals typically originate from a minority of sources—to embrace 80/20 thinking. This mindset isn't fixated on exact percentages; it's a strategic approach to nurturing top referral sources and discovering new ones. It involves engaging with current referral sources to expand your network to others with similar profiles.

When systematically gathering insights, you'll not only analyze data but also personally connect with referral sources. Interviewing those within and beyond the top 20 percent yields valuable perspectives. By starting with a foundation of at least three years of referral data, you create a robust platform for these discussions.

Then, you will examine the insights more closely and supplement them with interviews from other key stakeholders—clients and end users, such as patients or residents. This collective intelligence, coupled with the seasoned intuition of healthcare marketing professionals, leads to potent marketing strategies and narratives that resonate deeply.

With this rich tapestry of insights, the team builds targeted marketing recommendations that form a comprehensive growth marketing plan. This plan consists of actionable steps tailored to improve referral efforts and stimulate growth.

The process doesn't end with plan creation; it's cyclical. As insights evolve and marketing actions yield results, the strategy is continuously refined. Success breeds more success, turning the growth marketing plan into a dynamic, self-perpetuating flywheel.

And there's an additional dimension—a vital one—tying it all together: the art and science of storytelling. The power of narrative will be explored further in the next chapter, revealing how it's integral to transforming referral marketing strategies into reality.

5

LEVERAGE THE SCIENCE OF STORYTELLING

Did you grow up reading comic books, following the pursuits of Superman and Batman in Gotham City, or rooting for Spiderman and Iron Man fighting evil in New York City?

Filmmakers have certainly turned a love for comic books into a multibillion-dollar entertainment industry.

Growing up, a foray into creating comic books with my brother, Mike Mastovich, and our neighbor, Mike Mino, wasn't just child's play—it was a precursor to my professional ethos. These were my first collaborators in a lifelong pursuit of storytelling.

My youthful impatience—expecting Mike and Mike to transmute my thoughts into art—was an early lesson in communication and leadership. When they couldn't produce what was in my head, I'd scream and yell at them. Looking back years later, they probably thought, "Well, how can we possibly know exactly what's in your head when you're trying to tell us to draw Nuclear Man?"

Selling those homemade comics was more than a childhood hustle; it was the dawn of a holistic marketing mindset. It blended sales, storytelling, and marketing, an alchemy being unconsciously mastered. The journey continued through years of writing, speaking, and appearing on video, culminating during college—and beyond—in a profound appreciation for the science of storytelling.

STORYTELLING, THE CORNERSTONE OF MY CAREER

This fascination wasn't fleeting; it became a cornerstone of my career. Delving into the psychology of storytelling and understanding its power to engage, persuade, and inspire was key. This wasn't just art—it was a systematic application of narrative principles, a strategic layering of insights and creativity that propelled two radio stations from the bottom of the charts to the pinnacle of success.

From those early days of spirited direction to the nuanced understanding of storytelling's effect, my journey illustrates that effective communication is comprehensive. It's a tapestry woven from creativity, strategy, and a commitment to conveying the core message. That's the essence of no bullsh!t marketing—it's clear, purposeful, and always about connecting with the audience on a level that transcends the ordinary.

MOVING UP THE LADDER

Swapping my on-air role and the production booth for the manager's office was the turning point in my career. My new responsibilities took me from being the voice behind the mic to the one leading the charge, building a sales team, crafting promotional strategies, and directing a crew responsible for promotions and production. Leadership wasn't a role; it was the core of my approach, and effective communication was the key to this transition.

We didn't just climb from worst to first by chance; it was the ability to communicate our story compellingly to advertisers and fine-tune the radio formats to resonate with our desired audience. In those days, youthful confidence often led the way, allowing us to take bold steps that seasoned professionals might have hesitated to take. This was no bullsh!t marketing before it was called that—straightforward, honest, and successful.

Let's look at the first part, the science of storytelling, to potential advertisers. A legendary guy owned a jewelry store; he was the second generation of what ended up being four generations running the store. He was a pretty big advertiser and had been a previous client of the radio stations.

I came into the store and said hello, and he was nice, thinking maybe I was there to buy something. However, when I started explaining that I was from our radio stations, he said, "No, no." He started screaming, "No," pointing in my face and to the door. So, I left and returned the next day, and he did the same thing and threw me out again. On the third day, during his tirade, he started telling me a little bit of what had happened.

Some unscrupulous deals had occurred toward the end of the original stations' business dealings. The stations had offered a promotion he paid for, but they never ran it, let alone provided the desired results. The stations didn't deliver what was promised, and he was angry that they kept his money, but they never ran the promotion.

Returning to talk to him, I told him, "I understand what's happened to you." Repeating everything he told me and everything I had researched, I assured him, "Here's what I commit to you today. I'm here now. I'm building a team. We're turning this around. We're going to change the formats of the stations. We're going to promote the stations. We're going to win back the advertisers we have lost. I don't want your business today. I want you to know that I've made this commitment, and I will keep coming back and talking to you about our progress. And if you ever want to decide to be a part of it, that's great."

Framing that message and continuing to do that repeatedly with advertiser after advertiser ended up working, as there was some science to it. Regarding the target audience, the idea wasn't to go in and talk about the stations or me. What had happened to them was the most important information to uncover. What were their perceptions of the stations? Bad. What were some specific things that had happened? Awful. What did they like about our competition? The next step was to tell them how we were changing to do what they liked about the competition and to do even better advertising, and specific ways we would do that. Listening to them while not asking for any business was the science behind my method.

KNOW THE CORRECT STORY TO TELL

At the core of storytelling is making the audience the narrative's hero. Our minds are wired to engage with stories, instinctively crafting narratives where we seek the protagonist, their struggles, and their eventual triumph. This isn't just creative speculation; it's cognitive science. When you read this, you're not just scanning words; you're visualizing a journey, identifying with challenges, and anticipating resolutions.

As marketers, we must craft our messages to align with this natural storytelling arc. It's about framing the narrative to highlight the customer's challenges and hurdles and positioning ourselves as the ally equipped with solutions. This method isn't anecdotal; it's strategically grounded in how our brains process stories. It consists of ensuring that when we talk about our team, efforts, and victories, we do so in a way that resonates with this universal storytelling pattern. That's the backbone of storytelling science—a methodology applied consistently to forge connections and build trust.

We form stories every time we encounter others so why wouldn't we build our stories in the way the mind processes them?

We applied the science of storytelling across the board—from listener engagement promotions to enticing advertisers with programs like Christmas in July. Our programming and on-air talent were all tuned into this narrative approach. This wasn't just youthful bravado but strategic execution of proven principles.

Climbing the rankings from thirteenth and fourteenth to first and third was no fluke—it resulted from a systematic marketing strategy that transcended mere sales tactics. By leveraging storytelling, we connected with our audience, engaged them, and influenced their choices. This holistic approach was the engine behind our rise to the top, proving that when you harness the power of the story, you can turn even the most indifferent listeners and skeptical clients into your most ardent supporters.

PERSUADING WITH A STORY

Storytelling expert and former Forbes.com columnist Henry DeVries says: "Human brains are hardwired for stories."

In his book *Persuade With A Story!*,[5] he contends in the last fifteen years, neuroscience has proven that people make decisions not with the logical part of their brain but with the emotional part.

What is the shortest route to the emotional part of the brain? It's storytelling.

Building on this, cognitive science shows that when we interact with others, we automatically begin to formulate stories. We make someone the hero and want to understand the struggles they overcame, the barriers they faced, who helped them and how, and what lessons were learned. No Bullsh!t Story Building involves crafting your stories in the same way our minds are hardwired to process them.

Research supports that humans are wired to think in narratives. We instinctively perceive and process the world through stories in every encounter. We process information from each interaction in the form of a story, with one major takeaway or big idea.

Why, then, do we often fail to apply these principles in our business communications? If our brains are predisposed to create, understand, and retain stories, it stands to reason that our communication—both internal and external—should strive to leverage this natural inclination in the same format.

TOMMY APRYLE THROWS ME OUT BUT THROWS ME A LIFELINE

Sometimes, the lessons we need come wrapped in unexpected packages. Take Tommy Apryle, for instance, the guy from the jewelry store. His explosive reaction, with finger-pointing and loud accusations, could have ended any constructive conversation. But instead, it turned into a revelation.

Here's the deal: walking into Tommy's store, fresh-faced and ready to pitch, I had no idea there was a storm brewing from a past promotion gone wrong. It was Tommy, with his unmistakable bluntness, who opened my eyes. He didn't just throw me out that day, the next day, and the day after; he threw me a lifeline. Because of his forthrightness, a hidden issue costing us trust and business was discovered.

Armed with this newfound insight, the script was flipped. My pitches to other prospective clients now began by acknowledging past missteps and asking, "Has the so-called fantastic promotion burned you?" This approach resonated. It was authentic, direct, and acknowledged their frustration.

The result? We won back business, and more importantly, we earned our advertisers' trust. Out of the twelve companies left feeling shortchanged, each investing what would now amount to around $100,000, nearly all returned to our radio stations. We offered them a value they couldn't refuse: unused ad inventory, ensuring their message was heard far and wide, even in those 3 a.m. slots. We turned excess into opportunity.

So, as much as it hurt then, Tommy Apryle was the unsung hero of our turnaround. Although rough around the edges, his passion was exactly what we needed to hear. It wasn't just about the extra ads but about restoring faith. In the end, Tommy's business thrived with the surplus airtime, more than compensating for past disappointments.

In a way, Tommy Apryle's honesty catalyzed our success. He made us confront the uncomfortable truth, and in doing so, he helped us craft a strategy that turned a loss into a win—for everyone involved.

Tommy was the hero of that story for this reason. When you get punched in the mouth like Tyson said, you think, OK, was that person completely (or partially) insane, or was there some merit to what they expressed? Most of the time, they have some merit. Although I know this now, at that young age, I came home bitching and moaning, then went drinking with my buddies to let out my frustrations.

THE CHIRO JOE REVELATION

Feedback has transformative power, even when delivered with a sting. I learned this firsthand through an experience that revolutionized how I presented deliverables to our clients.

Chiro Joe, a chiropractor with a fiery passion for his practice, couldn't visualize the potential of our messaging across different media. Our typical approach was to lay out the messaging strategy—the big idea and storytelling pillars—as part of the initial engagement. Ensuing meetings would involve creating and demonstrating the content beyond that, such as videos, blogs, website copy, search engine marketing, etc. However, too often, this left clients nodding in agreement during the first presentation, only to become paralyzed and indecisive for a time afterward. It was like serving a gourmet meal to someone without providing the cutlery—they appreciated the look but couldn't dig in.

Joe let loose a torrent of frustration in a meeting filled with his staff and mine. "I don't think I like this. What does this stuff even mean? You guys say you're no BS, but I think this is BS." Despite his abrasive approach, a lightbulb went off. Joe, in his less-than-diplomatic manner, was pointing out a blind spot. He was challenging us not just to create and present a company's storytelling tagline and overall framework in the first engagement's big reveal but also to showcase the marketing approach in action with some specific tactical marketing actions.

We took Joe's rant as a challenge. Stepping into our clients' shoes, we dramatized our strategies in mock-up BombBomb videos, social media posts, emails, and blog entries—all rough around the edges but vibrant and tangible. When we unveiled this dynamic presentation to Joe, his tirade turned to praise. "This! This is what I wanted to see!" he exclaimed.

Joe's outburst became a catalyst for change. We realized that every client, especially those unfamiliar with the intricacies of growth marketing, needed to see their story come to life beyond their big idea and supporting storytelling pillars, even in the first engagement. They needed to feel the pulse of their message across various platforms immediately, even if the examples weren't what we'd see as an actual finished product. Thanks to Chiro Joe, we ensure clients can touch and taste the fruits of their messaging within weeks of their first engagement with us.

So, while Chiro Joe's methods were unorthodox, his impact was undeniable. He unknowingly became the hero of our process improvement, teaching us a vital lesson in client engagement. It was a stark reminder that sometimes, the most valuable insights come from the most unexpected places—and heroes can emerge even when they're giving you a piece of their mind.

WHERE WE ARE GOING NEXT

Storytelling is vital, but there is also something else that is critical. That something else is the marketing mindset, the topic of the following chapter.

6

CULTIVATE A MARKETING MINDSET

Throughout life, some people enter your world at just the right moment, making a significant impact. As a junior in college, I encountered a young professor, Krish Krishnan, who was vibrant and far from the traditional stodgy academic.

He introduced the class to simulations and marketing insights that were ahead of their time. A few years later, while my team and I were turning around radio stations, Krishnan, then the dean of an MBA program, reached out to me.

His proposition was straightforward yet innovative: he wanted to build the graduate program with young, successful alums, offering me a dual opportunity—an assistantship and a job that included working at the Small Business Institute, collaborating with professors on books, and engaging in market research. MBAs weren't as common back then, so this was a big deal.

Despite the financial success I enjoyed at the time—a point of pride for someone my age—I chose to take a risk. Leaving a lucrative job and partially offsetting the pay cut with DJ gigs and media work, I made a fraction of what I had previously earned. But this decision wasn't about income. It was a strategic move back into an educational "lab" setting, where what I'd learned in business could be applied to help small and midsize companies at the Institute while diving into graduate studies.

During this period, I collaborated with various small and midsize businesses to tackle issues from workers' compensation to employee health insurance. Our projects made waves, even becoming finalists for the US Small Business Administration Consulting Project of the Year award. Simultaneously, I was absorbing everything I could about employee healthcare and the complexities of managing costs for small and medium-sized businesses.

A PRESIDENTIAL DEBATE LEADS TO AN EPIPHANY

Then came a pivotal moment—watching a 1992 presidential debate between President George H. W. Bush and Governor Bill Clinton. Clinton's focus on the healthcare problem, emphasizing the need for "managed care," resonated with me. I realized that my upcoming MBA positioned me perfectly for the anticipated demand for healthcare-focused MBAs.

This isn't just my story. It illustrates a fundamental truth: when we're open to opportunities and willing to take calculated risks, we align our path with the broader currents of change, ready to meet the future head-on.

Then, sure enough, I landed a role with a healthcare

system focused on branding and storytelling. They were keen to expand beyond their main hospital. Their strategy to reach local business leaders? An occupational medicine program aimed at helping local employers minimize injuries and expedite recovery would create a pathway for additional services like MRIs or surgeries and a foot in the door when the system was ready to roll out its own health insurance product.

I brought my experience from the radio stations alongside the marketing wisdom of my mentor, Philip Kotler, to the role—though modified with real-world knocks. I tackled the challenge from both angles: business-to-consumer, connecting with patients, and business-to-business, engaging employers.

The presidential debate did indeed herald a transformation in healthcare, ushering in an era of "managed care." The industry began to value business savvy, particularly in hospital management—a sector previously run more like independent entities than businesses. Marketing, once a term almost taboo to doctors and hospital administrators, became integral.

We cultivated a marketing mindset within the healthcare system, which then radiated outwards. This approach, seeded by a national debate, has been a cornerstone, demonstrating the profound impact of viewing healthcare through a marketer's lens.

Adopting a marketing mindset necessitates a fundamental shift in perspective, especially in healthcare. Historically, the industry didn't center around the end user—the patient.

Recall hospitals from the mid-twentieth century to the mid-1990s; they resembled scenes from *The Godfather* where Don Corleone is hospitalized, and Michael and Enzo the Baker pretend to be the muscle guarding the hospital.[6]

Hospitals at that time were foreboding, not customer-centric. That's how hospitals were. They were a place to go to when you were sick or dying.

We needed to and could change that.

I pushed for a "wayfinding" system to help people—whether actual patients or friends and family visiting them—when entering the healthcare facility. The term was met with blank stares until it was explained that we needed a system to help people quickly and easily find their way around the hospital from the parking garage to one place and then to the next place.

Undeterred by the initial response, we pushed forward, finding a specialist who would later help revolutionize navigation within multiple health systems, making them more customer-friendly.

That was necessary because hospitals back then didn't focus on what patients, their families, and friends wanted. Instead, they provided what was deemed necessary. This isn't wrong in itself—delivering critical care is essential. However, complaints about the food, the parking, and difficulty navigating hospital corridors were commonplace.

These grievances often overshadowed the quality of the medical care received. It's telling when the takeaway from a life-saving service is "The food was terrible," or "The staff were unfriendly," or "My family got lost trying to find me." This is not what anyone expects from a place where lives are saved.

The entire industry needed a shift toward a marketing mindset.

7

TAKE A LESSON FROM HIGHER EDUCATION

During my tenure at UPMC, the environment was challenging despite the success. Then, an acquaintance mentioned a senior communications and marketing leadership position at a university going through a turnaround. Initially, I shrugged it off, content at the big player UPMC. However, the university struggled to fill the role as time passed, and UPMC's internal dynamics grew even more contentious. When a couple of university board leaders reached out about a year later, the timing and the opportunity felt different.

During discussions, I had moments of hesitation, including a candid dinner with the university president where my job details were outlined and what it would take financially was discussed. My worth was known, and the required resources for me to make a real impact were in place. The president needed time to consider, and when he returned, it was with an offer that nearly met my terms. When I held firm on my end, they finally agreed to meet my conditions fully for both a compensation package and equally important from a marketing budget and resources standpoint.

PROVING THE PROCESS IN ANOTHER INDUSTRY
SIMILAR TO HEALTHCARE

My observation that higher education was on the cusp of transformation, similar to the one healthcare had undergone a decade prior, influenced my decision to shift industries. Both sectors were riddled with independent fiefdoms, a lack of marketing insight, and a crucial commonality: unlike most purchases, in both cases, the end user often didn't pay the full amount (or sometimes even any of the amount) charged for the service. In healthcare, it was mostly employers or the government who paid the tab; in higher education, it was primarily parents, grants, or scholarships. Additionally, the university I joined faced a demographic decline in its traditional recruitment areas, a trend that necessitated expanding its reach to ensure sustainability.

Recognizing these parallels, I saw an opportunity to inject a robust marketing mindset into higher education, employing strategies that had been successful in healthcare. This was a chance to validate the impact of comprehensive growth marketing in another vital, evolving industry.

We revolutionized storytelling at the university by anchoring it in science-driven artistry. We launched a vast market research study, engaging with a spectrum of stakeholders—prospective and current students, applicants who had been accepted but declined, parents of each group, community leaders, alumni, university staff, and faculty—to reshape our narrative. This research led to our creation of a fresh tagline, redefined storytelling pillars, and even a revamped logo, addressing the challenge of name recognition and difficult pronunciation beyond the region surrounding the university.

Our mandate was to extend our reach beyond the familiar confines of the immediate region, which had an aging and declining population, and project our message statewide, nationally, and internationally. We crafted a message that aligned with the aspirations of both parents and students, tailoring it across the university's ten schools and creating a unified yet distinct campaign.

Mirroring the success strategies from healthcare, we targeted admissions with precision marketing, segmented our audiences, and leveraged the strengths of a diligent admissions team and supportive leadership. The results were undeniable—consecutive years of record-breaking first-year classes, not only in size but also in academic talent.

It's crucial to credit the teamwork throughout the university and the entire leadership team. My role was to steer the growth strategy and oversee its execution. This collaborative success story underscored the power of a well-devised, well-executed marketing strategy in transforming an institution's reach and reputation and proved that the growth marketing strategies that worked in healthcare could succeed in another industry.

RESEARCH BECOMES AN IMPORTANT TOOL

In market research, striving for perfection often impedes the good.

When resources are tight, qualitative methods can yield rich insights. At UPMC, our budget allowed for extensive qualitative and quantitative research, but in other situations, we adapted, combining focus groups and one-on-one interviews with broader surveys to balance depth with breadth.

At the university, for example, we conducted dozens of interviews and a comprehensive campus-wide survey, providing a robust mix of qualitative and quantitative data. This blend allowed for a thorough understanding of the numbers and the stories behind them.

Telephone interviews offered qualitative insights with open-ended questions, while written and email surveys delivered quantitative data. Echoing Lord Kelvin, unmeasured knowledge is unsatisfactory, but practical insights are gold.[7]

Lloyd Corder, a strategic partner of mine since I was at UPMC, is a champion of the snapshot survey. The snapshot survey is the opposite of what most people think of when they hear the term survey research. By asking a limited sample of your target audience a set of highly focused questions, the snapshot survey gives you valuable insights in just a few days—not in weeks or months—at a fraction of the cost.

Corder's book, *The Snapshot Survey: Quick, Affordable Marketing Research for Every Organization*,[8] advocates for speedy and cost-effective research, delivering results in days, not weeks—a timely and effective approach we leveraged starting at UPMC and continue to use today.

When it comes to research, it's about using the right tool for the job and ensuring your knowledge is robust, actionable, and grounded in reality.

From the research comes message strategies. An important group to tell your culture story to are employees, and it pays to simplify the message. The next chapter examines ways to do that.

8

SIMPLIFY THE MESSAGE FOR EMPLOYEES

Do you recall the film *Apollo 13*?

This Academy Award–winning Hollywood drama starring Tom Hanks is based on the events of the 1970 Apollo 13 lunar mission, during which astronauts Jim Lovell, Fred Haise, and Jack Swigert found everything going according to plan after leaving Earth's orbit.

However, when an oxygen tank exploded, the scheduled moon landing was called off. Numerous technical problems threatened both the astronauts' survival and their safe return to Earth.

In what has been called NASA's finest hour, a team of engineers back on Earth designed a solution using an odd collection of spare parts to save the Apollo 13 crew from certain death.

MY COMPANY'S FINEST HOUR

While the stakes were not as high, I can relate to how those NASA engineers must have felt.

A challenge we faced reminded me of the square-peg-into-a-round-hole scene from the movie *Apollo 13*. After the Apollo 13 spacecraft suffered the explosion, mission control's engineers dumped duplicates of all the items found on the spaceship onto a table. The leader tells the team they must use these pieces to create something that works to get the astronauts home.[9]

And they do.

Let's dive into how my marketing firm, MASSolutions, transformed Medicare research into a practical growth strategy for a growing Medicare Advantage program. We knew the new Chief Marketing Officer of the health plan and respected his journey from a call center position to chief marketing officer, which was a testament to his dedication and understanding of the job from the ground up.

The CMO had inherited over twenty studies packed with insights on the Medicare Advantage consumer, leading to a classic case of analysis paralysis among employees.

He brought out a jumbled mess of data, seeking clarity for the marketing team, call center staff, operations, and the C-suite. The information overload was like handing someone a dense book on a topic they barely knew—a daunting and impractical task. This challenge exemplified the essence of no bullsh!t marketing: a unique project that could significantly shift a client's trajectory.

We distilled the studies into a concise, compelling narrative, honing in on five key themes, and condensed the findings into an impactful deck of slides. Each slide featured a striking image or a couple of potent bullet points. This approach sparked the marketing team's "aha" moments, allowing them to grasp, sell, and implement the insights through effective B2E communication strategies, affecting everything from storytelling to operations.

The CMO emerged as the hero in this story. With the insight to recognize there was a treasure trove of knowledge buried under the clutter, he sought our expertise. We delivered, and he boldly presented the streamlined strategy to the CEO, who came on board. This wasn't our solo effort—the CMO had the foresight and confidence to realize the need for change and the leadership to make it happen.

OUR APOLLO 13 MOMENT

When faced with another similar challenge—a health insurer had been sending nearly forty pieces of marketing materials and forms to potential new members, hoping they could sort through them and sign up—we took a stand. We called out the clutter and transformed it into a singular, effective communication piece.

Now, I do not have delusions of grandeur. We certainly weren't in a life-or-death situation when helping the health insurer. But we did have a bunch of stuff that we had to simplify and turn into something that would get us the response we wanted.

We tackled the heap of information, hoping to spark some ingenuity like those NASA engineers did.

In the boardroom, we laid out all the marketing materials before the leadership team, a stark visualization of the clutter akin to the scattered hardware on the Apollo 13 engineers' table. Some pieces even slid off the table onto the floor, unintentionally emphasizing our point—this was information overload and ineffective.

From this chaotic assortment, we designed a streamlined, single piece of communication, a blueprint for clear messaging that would resonate with potential members. Just as the Apollo 13 engineers had to guide astronauts verbally through the makeshift fix, we systematically gathered insights to ensure that our message was heard, understood, and acted upon by members and employees alike.

This mission wasn't about surviving a crisis but transforming a scattered approach into a focused, successful strategy that resonated with its audience—proving that you can solve the problem and achieve the storytelling goal with the right team and approach.

This approach was about homing in on what truly mattered. In the sea of information, we sought the lighthouse— what do members need to know, considering their limited time and attention? We gathered insights systematically, asking members directly to identify the crux of their needs.

The Apollo 13 analogy brought the message home for the leadership team. Spilling a box of thirty-seven marketing pieces was a visual cue of information overload. The key takeaway: simplicity wins. By trimming the fat and focusing on what's essential, online and traditional channels can work harmoniously, delivering the message without overwhelming the audience. This strategy wasn't just about cutting costs—it was about cutting through the noise to resonate with our audience effectively.

SHIFT YOUR MARKETING MINDSET TO CURRENT EMPLOYEES

For some reason, companies struggle to realize the importance of marketing to talent acquisition and retention. When we talk with CEOs about their current employees, we hammer home the point about the importance of marketing to their teams. It's about crafting messages that speak directly to current and potential team members, utilizing the channels they're already on, and segmenting the workforce to deliver these messages effectively.

Pushback comes in statements such as, "Look, we pay them, we offer benefits, we recognize their efforts—and now you're saying we need a full-blown marketing plan for them? Like we're trying to woo new customers?" It doesn't come naturally to view current employees as a target market worthy of specific marketing campaigns.

But here's the rub: it's not just a "maybe we'll try

that." It's essential. When you connect with your employees and make them the focus of targeted marketing efforts, you invest in your company's culture and success. Communicating effectively with your team—whether full or part-time employees or contract workers—fosters a productive environment where every team member feels they're an integral part of the big picture. When you get this right, it's like adding jet fuel to your company's engine. Most companies don't get it right because they don't commit to investing time and money in real B2E marketing.

A prime example is a large continuing care retirement community (CCRC) that was grappling with growth issues. They had a solid reputation, but something was off. They asked us to systematically gather insights and leverage our experience, expertise, and instincts to find and outline a solution. We found the crux of the problem through qualitative and quantitative research and spending time observing the customer journey.

The problem was not related to compassionate care or the latest technology. It wasn't tied to amenities or service offerings. It came down to the overall experience for both prospective residents and the families of current residents. Whether dropping in to see family or scoping out the place for potential residency, visitors often arrived at empty reception areas during peak hours—lunchtime and late afternoon.

The administrative staff, long-tenured and set in their ways, would all break for lunch simultaneously, leaving the front desk unstaffed. The same scenario unfolded toward the end of the day. So, we pitched an idea to the VP of marketing that could tackle multiple issues at once.

Here was our plan: introduce a concierge program akin to a Walmart greeter that wouldn't cost extra but would enhance the visitor experience. Employees from various departments would step into this role during peak times, maybe just an hour a month, covering for each other. This way, they'd experience firsthand what visitors and potential clients encounter, absorbing the feedback and questions, essentially becoming the eyes and ears of the community.

We knew this approach could provide that warm welcome during busy times and elevate each employee's understanding of the community beyond their usual role. It was a simple yet ingenious shift in routine that promised to inject a new perspective into their work.

The VP took a leap of faith and ran with our suggestion, which paid off. Despite initial concerns about coverage during these staff absences, each department adapted, and the concierge program flourished. Employees became more than their job titles; they became ambassadors and storytellers, bridging their regular duties with broader community outreach.

The impact was significant. That year, the VP was awarded "Employee of the Year"—a nod to the innovative approach that MASSolutions helped to implement at this expansive CCRC. While the VP was ready to credit us, it was the VP's vision that brought this transformation to life—a testament to the power of a simple, well-executed idea that turned employees into engaged, multifaceted contributors to the community's growth and success.

This success at the CCRC exemplifies the crux of no bullsh!t marketing:

- *Identifying every key audience:* The CCRC had overlooked crucial groups: the families of current and potential residents and, not least, their own employees. Recognizing each audience's significance is step one.

- *Understanding and meeting needs:* These groups needed guidance during peak visit times. We pinpointed this need and addressed it head-on—no more aimless wandering for visitors during those critical hours.

- *Consistent communication:* Rolling out the concierge program wasn't a one-and-done announcement. We crafted a robust plan to keep everyone informed, repeatedly reinforcing the message both within the community and beyond its borders.

- *Prioritizing employees:* B2E marketing isn't an afterthought. It's about communicating with current and potential employees with the same vigor you pursue your external customers. Develop targeted B2E marketing campaigns to reach, connect, and engage with them and tell your culture story again and again. Your team is the backbone of your operation; when team members thrive, so does the business.

Ultimately, it concerns respect and recognition—ensuring every person who interacts with your organization feels valued and understood, whether they're part of your staff or the community you serve. It's straightforward, sincere, and strategic.

Next, we'll outline how you can ask the right questions to find out what you need to know to drive growth.

9

JUST ASK YOURSELF THE RIGHT QUESTIONS

Are you asking the right (or any) questions about who is referring to you?

In an era when information is at our fingertips, and decision-makers are inundated with pitches, it's the questions we ask that set us apart. It's like when you're scrolling through your favorite streaming service, searching for the next binge-worthy show. The algorithm suggests options based on what you've watched, but the real gem, the show that becomes your next obsession, is often discovered through a deeper dive and asking: "What am I really in the mood for? What haven't I seen?"

That's what it's like when you ask: "Who has been referring to me and why? And who could be referring to me, and why aren't they?"

The right answers might be worth millions, as this story illustrates.

WON THE BUSINESS WHILE DRIVING

My parents taught me the importance of asking questions and the power of listening. This lesson was only reinforced in my media career, where asking the right questions, pausing to listen, and then probing deeper became fundamental to success. This approach has been pivotal at every stop in my journey—from radio stations to healthcare and beyond.

Using this story as an example: We were competing for a large multi-physician group's business. They were looking for expertise in marketing strategy and branding. After several recommendations, they whittled down the options, and we were in the mix. However, scheduling conflicts arose, and the opportunity began to slip away. So, a call was scheduled when I knew I'd be driving—a risk, but necessary.

The CEO of the physician group organization recalls an initial impression of me being distracted. However, delving into question after question, they began to see the method in what might have seemed like madness. The questions weren't just good; they were necessary, uncovering aspects of their business they hadn't considered. It shifted the dynamic entirely.

The CEO said, "I realized Dave wasn't distracted. He was quite focused. He was asking all these questions and all the others had come into it telling—they were selling and telling. As soon as the call started, the others would all say, 'We do this, we do that, we've worked with this physician group.' Dave's approach was different, allowing him to learn more about our business.

"And then, finally, we said, 'Hey, we only have a few minutes left. Can you tell us what you would do?' And he returned and said, 'Well, I have enough information now. I've learned enough to say you have this particular challenge, which we've worked on a lot, but I need to find out more by doing this and that so we'd have more insights. And then we'd come back and build your marketing plan. It would be comprehensive, and we'd build your storytelling around what we learned.'" The CEO hung up and then said, "Hey, we've talked to eight people. That's the one."

Where others were busy selling, I was inquiring, listening, and understanding. When finally asked what would be done, I could outline a preliminary strategy tailored to their challenges based on real insights from our conversation. It wasn't just about what we could offer but what they needed and how we could help. That focus, that clarity of purpose, won us the business. We've been working with them ever since because asking the right questions, listening intently, and following up aren't just marketing strategies; they're life strategies.

We got the business and helped them achieve their growth goals through marketing and storytelling. The CEO and I are still friends to this day.

USING THE DATA

When it comes to referral source marketing, the data angle is crucial. Many healthcare organizations have a blind spot here—they're great at collecting data for billing and operations, and that's critical, no question about it. But where they often miss a beat is capturing data through a marketing lens, data that could enhance the customer journey and inform their marketing and storytelling. It's not about reinventing the wheel; it's about making subtle shifts in data collection to reveal insights that can make a real difference.

Here's where asking the right questions comes into play. You need to look at your data and ask, "What's this telling me about my customers? How can this improve their experience?" It's about complementing the operational data with a layer of customer-focused insights and painting a full picture that combines the hard numbers with the human experience.

And then there's the power of 80/20 thinking—a mindset about efficiency and impact. Look at your referral sources; around 20 percent are likely responsible for 80 percent of your patients. That's a gold mine of insight waiting to be tapped. You need to sit down with these top referrers and ask them pointedly, "What's the one reason you refer to us?" This single question can unveil what sets you apart in their minds, helping you understand and amplify your strengths.

By integrating this 80/20 principle into your questioning, you're not just gathering data but homing in on the most influential data. This approach doesn't cast a wide net with the hope of catching something meaningful—it's targeted, strategic, and designed to give you actionable insights that can dramatically refine your marketing and storytelling efforts. That's no bullsh!t marketing—data-driven, customer-focused, and always asking the right questions.

Asking the tough questions about data—the kind that others might not think to ask or don't have the answers to immediately—and then using the data enables you to see things more clearly than your competitors.

Here's how it goes. Our clients are told, "We'll sign any nondisclosure agreement necessary, but we need to dig into three years of your data." That data, whether sales figures, patient stats, or revenue details, is gold. It's how we pinpoint the client's best customers, who they might be, and who they should be. This is about getting to the heart of the business and understanding the essence of the current state to map out where the client is headed.

Marketing isn't about fancy campaigns; it's about driving results that matter—top-line growth, bottom-line efficiency, and fostering personal and professional development of team members.

Anyone promising guarantees without a deep dive into the data is selling you hot air. True marketing finesse comes from interpreting a range of data points to craft strategies that are as informed as they are creative.

THE POWER OF ANALOGIES IN STORYTELLING

This chapter started with a story for a reason.

Let me underscore the significance of anecdotes and analogies; they're the dynamite in your storytelling tool kit. Stories are particularly potent once you've delved deep, extracting vital insights from your key target markets and finding out what they really think about your product or service.

Sift through all you've heard and choose the snippets that will reverberate because spinning those anecdotes and analogies into vivid tales will spark your audience's imagination.

Here's a slice of MASSolutions in action, proof that we practice what we preach. Consider this pitch with the head honcho of a bespoke furniture enterprise. The guy wanted proof—a recent taste of success. So, we told a story about a home medical equipment provider, specifically their quest to amplify their oxygen therapy referrals. "In six short months," I said, "we doubled their O_2 referrals."

That's when the room lit up. "That's it! That's what I'm after. Double my O_2 referrals!" he exclaimed. And just like that, the story resonated, the analogy stuck, and we had ourselves a deal. Even though he sold bespoke furniture, he'd remind us every few weeks, "Double those O_2s!"

The funny thing is, that became more than just a sign-up tale. It evolved into a mantra for our team, "Double the O_2s for the furniture folks!" It's a testament that the right story, told well, isn't just memorable. It motivates, it sticks, and it becomes part of your DNA.

Remember, whether it's O_2s or ottomans, the right anecdote at the right time can be the spark that ignites action and commitment. Use them wisely, and watch your stories become the stuff of legends.

You will want to use specific anecdotes with specific referral sources. Next, we will examine the importance of multiple referral source segments and strategies to engage each group.

10

USE MULTIPLE REFERRAL SOURCES IN A SYSTEMATIC WAY

Imagine a master chef who blends common spices into an extraordinary signature dish. Individually, these spices might add a hint of flavor, but combined with skill and precision, they create a culinary sensation that's far more valuable than the sum of its parts.

That's what we did. We mixed the insights from filling up an assisted living facility into a recipe for success for our clients. I'm here to show you how to blend your own ingredients—your referral sources—into a gourmet strategy that's both satisfying and profitable.

MASSOLUTIONS IS MORE THAN A NAME—IT IS A PHILOSOPHY

Our philosophy is about the magic of tapping into the power of referrals from physicians, surgeons, hospital case managers, social service agencies, and other sources for clients across the healthcare space.

While driving change at the healthcare system, "assisted living" became the buzzword. We were trying to wrap our heads around it and saw an opportunity. We teamed up with a partner who knew the ropes of managing these communities. With our marketing chops and their operational expertise, we filled up faster than they'd ever seen.

We targeted potential residents, their adult children, and those all-important referral sources, dusting off the old playbook with a fresh twist. Hospital case managers, social service agencies like the Area Agency on Aging, and primary care physicians all had the potential to send folks our way.

Our systematic marketing approach sealed the deal: referral source marketing, segmentation, and direct consumer outreach. We knew who to talk to—residents, their families, and the referral sources. And that's where the questions come in, the kind that get you to the nitty-gritty of who's sending residents your way and why—or why not.

Fast-forward to when I'm working at another big healthcare system, and some leaders from that assisted living vendor set out to start their own assisted living management company. They valued my marketing, selling, and storytelling skills and pitched me to join as a partner. Working in an industry where our customers' life span was typically eighteen to twenty months wasn't appealing. That would be tough, as I thrive on variety in challenging new sectors.

They countered with a consulting offer, so I started diving into projects, shaping strategies, and rolling out segmentation. Then, out of the blue, they called me and said, "Dave, we have a problem." I got nervous and wondered what went wrong, so I picked up the phone and called the CEO. He said: "Dave, you need to bill us." That's when it hit me—a name for this gig was needed. I sat down with Mike Mino, that childhood neighbor who became a creative design expert, and my brother, Mike Mastovich, a nationally recognized writer. We toss around ideas and land on MASSolutions.

Senior living had a different dynamic compared to other healthcare sectors. Direct self-referrals from residents or their children were higher, but we could never underestimate the influence of a trusted doctor or social worker. They might make up a smaller slice of the pie, but it's crucial. With that first client, we demonstrated the full MASSolutions approach—healthcare referral sources, branding, direct-to-consumer, strategic KPIs—and it all started with asking the right questions and then listening intently to what the data was whispering.

Fortunately, our approach works in almost every healthcare industry sector.

Now comes the task of creating multiple stories for multiple targets, which is explored in the following chapter.

11

STORIES FOR MULTIPLE TARGETS

Imagine your brand's core message as a tree: solid, singular, deeply rooted. From that one trunk, branches grow in different directions, each supporting leaves that catch the light uniquely. Every branch is a storytelling pillar, reaching out to different audiences, but all are connected back to the central idea—the sturdy trunk.

In a landscape where marketing often imitates the short-lived blossoming of flowers, I advocate for the enduring growth akin to trees. It's about establishing a brand message that, like a trunk, remains steadfast amid the changing seasons of industry trends and consumer behaviors.

Simon Sinek captured the imaginations of leaders and marketers worldwide with a similar natural analogy in his celebrated book, *Start With Why*.[10] He explored how influential figures and organizations ground their actions and communications in a powerful "why"—their purpose, cause, or belief.

While Sinek's viral TEDx Talk[11] and book tap into the "why" as an organizational beacon, my approach expands upon this to focus on not just one but two "why" questions: your why or reason for being and your customers' why or reason for buying. Both should intertwine seamlessly like the roots and branches of a robust tree.

Take this case from my experience: a client had a lofty mission focused on their employees' well-being. They were telling their clients that their employees came first. Even though many people now might say they care about the employees at the places they're buying from, it's still not something most customers want to hear front and center. We naturally want to be the focal point when we are customers. So, while the intentions were good, this mission statement's appeal to their clientele met with skepticism. We needed a message that resonated across the spectrum, from employees to clients and beyond.

We reshaped their narrative into a cohesive statement that spoke volumes to each target market. We evolved their altruistic core into a three-dimensional focus that stood the test of time, encapsulating the essence of improving lives for employees, residents, and their families. When you nail the narrative with your why or reason for being and your customers' why or reason for buying, it transcends the message—it becomes a mission that resonates with everyone it touches.

We embody this practice at MASSolutions, too. "Bold solutions, no BS" isn't just a catchy slogan—it's a living philosophy that resonates with our current and potential employees, customers, and partners. It's about authenticity and results, attracting those who share our ethos and deterring those who don't.

For our team, it's the standard we live by and the mea-sure by which we hold ourselves accountable. For potential recruits, it signals a culture of transparency and drive. And for our referral sources, it's a badge of integrity that they're proud to associate with.

Here's a why for you: Why not apply the same strate-gic understanding and growth marketing savvy you use to enchant external customers to mesmerize your internal ones? The next chapter examines that.

12

REVAMP YOUR B2E MARKETING PERIODICALLY

Consider this a cycle of success:

- Engaged employees lead to satisfied patients, who, along with their doctors, become the referral sources we spoke of earlier.

- The engagement, loyalty, and advocacy of your employees is where true transformation begins.

- Weaving together referral source and B2E marketing isn't just smart; it's essential.

B2E marketing is about talent acquisition and employee retention because every piece of the puzzle, every department, and every individual contributes to the masterpiece we call brand success. And in this masterpiece, every stroke, every color, every nuance matters. That's the essence of no bullsh!t marketing—holistic, inclusive, and real.

Let's champion this cause with the tenacity it deserves, turning our organizations into bastions of excellence where every employee is an advocate, every patient a story of success, and every referral a testament to our unwavering commitment to health and the customer experience. B2E Marketing makes your company a destination employer that takes your talent acquisition to another level.

TEST, TRACK, AND TWEAK YOUR B2E MARKETING

To stay ahead, especially in today's hybrid work world, businesses must treat their internal marketing with the same vigor and strategic thinking as they do their external marketing.

Talk to C-level executives and you're likely to hear that their primary challenge is attracting and retaining top talent in this new, complex work environment. A robust, periodically revamped B2E strategy is key to meeting that challenge head-on and securing the talent necessary to execute the strategies we are crafting.

Embracing a B2E marketing approach can revolutionize how businesses view their current and potential employees. It's a shift in perspective, aligning with marketing and storytelling strategies that spotlight the value and contributions of each team member.

The initial commitment to a B2E framework is a leap forward, but it's just the beginning. Like any robust marketing effort, it demands evolution—constant refinement and adaptability.

Here's where the mantra "test, track, and tweak" becomes a pillar of the process. It's about examining your B2E strategies, evaluating their effectiveness, and adjusting accordingly.

This continuous improvement cycle applies not just to your customer-facing initiatives but also to your internal ones. After all, your employees are your first line of ambassadors.

Take, for instance, the case of a company in a notoriously high-turnover industry. They came to us with a staggering turnover rate among their five hundred–person workforce. We introduced a B2E marketing philosophy and a cultural mindset shift that revamped how they engaged with their team and potential employees during recruitment. The turnover rate plummeted within two years, landing well below the industry average.

But success isn't a signal to coast; it's a cue for the next act. Eighteen months in, it was time to reevaluate and reinvigorate the B2E strategy. By examining what had worked and what hadn't and introducing fresh ideas and channels, we kicked off another round of successful engagement.

This renewal cycle has been repeated multiple times, ensuring that the company's B2E efforts never grow stale but remain dynamic and effective.

When done correctly, systematic B2E marketing efforts produce a certain momentum. In the next chapter, we compare them to a piece of machinery called a flywheel.

13

DEVELOP YOUR FLYWHEEL

In the world of transformative success stories, Amazon stands tall—a colossus that's reshaped our lives and continues to do so.

Amazon's secret? The idea began with a scribble on a napkin, the blueprint of what would become a colossal flywheel, a concept brilliantly unpacked in Jim Collins's *Good To Great*.[12] His book transcends time, age, and industry; its lessons are perennially pertinent.

BEHOLD THE FLYWHEEL

The flywheel is a heavy revolving wheel in a machine that is used to increase the machine's momentum. The flywheel in machinery smooths out the operational kinks, and it's much the same for a business. This produces a synergy of processes, people, and products that, once set in motion, keeps accelerating growth and driving market share, customer acquisition, and profit.

Lower Prices
on
More Offerings

Grow
Revenues per
Fixed Costs

**Amazon.com
Flywheel**

Increase
Customer
Visits

Expand the Store,
Extend Distribution

Attract
Third-Party
Sellers

With its obsessive focus on low costs, vast choice, and a sprawling seller base, Amazon's flywheel creates an unstoppable momentum that continually attracts more customers. As their numbers swell, so does Amazon's ability to slash prices further, beckon more sellers, bolster choice, and lure more customers. It's a perpetual cycle of growth, a master class in strategy.

But it's not just for the Amazons of the world. The flywheel concept is a crucible where marketing, operational, and organizational strategies meld. It's a strategic trifecta that many claim to wield, but few truly grasp. And here's where many falter: conflating strategy with mere tactics. The flywheel's beauty lies in its holistic approach, integrating the various facets of strategy to propel the company forward.

Amazon's flywheel wasn't just about being the low-cost leader. It was about breadth of choice, seller diversity, and customer volume—a formula for scale and dominance. Your business has a unique opportunity to craft a flywheel that aligns your marketing efforts with organizational structure, operational efficiency, and financial strategy. It's a holistic model that can drive exponential growth.

It's important to grasp that the concept of strategy is multifaceted. Strategy isn't a one-size-fits-all approach; it's divided into organizational, financial, and marketing strands. Organizational strategy shapes your company's structure, leadership, and management style. Financial strategy determines your fiscal approach. A marketing strategy identifies your target customers and how to connect and engage with them by delivering what they want, when and where they want it, at a price they're willing to pay.

Unfortunately, strategy often becomes a buzzword, tossed around to mean everything and nothing. True strategic thinking goes beyond mere tactics. It's about understanding the interplay among different types of strategies and leveraging them for growth.

This is where the flywheel shines. It's not just a piece of machinery; it's a holistic framework that propels your company forward. It ensures every aspect of your business—from operations to customer engagement—constantly works harmoniously to improve your core objectives.

Your business's flywheel should encompass your marketing strategy, focusing on who your customers are, what they want, and how to deliver value in their desired ways. This approach isn't about selling but building relationships and stories that resonate with your customers. It's about creating a narrative that meets their needs and entices them back, time and again.

By adopting a flywheel mindset, you commit to a strategy seeking exponential growth through operational and marketing synergy. It's an ongoing cycle of understanding, delivering, communicating, and enhancing—all tailored to your customers' evolving needs.

As you reflect on this, consider how each segment of your strategy contributes to the flywheel's momentum. The goal is not just to sell but to create an ecosystem where each success breeds further success, all aligned with your company's vision and customers' desires.

Now, let's go behind the scenes of MASSolutions' flywheel. Our journey starts with systematic insight gathering—the bedrock of marketing science. We dive deep into qualitative and quantitative data, segment markets, analyze competitors and your sales data, and leverage tools like the Predictive Index (PI)—a brief assessment of what energizes and drains a person—to understand the motivations behind behaviors. The insights gleaned are the fuel for our flywheel.

MASSOLUTIONS FLYWHEEL

Systematically
Gather
Insights

Change
Behaviors
& Mindsets

**MASSolutions
Flywheel**

Leverage Experience,
Expertise, Instincts

Reach, Connect,
Engage Audiences

Develop Solutions,
Create Stories

With these insights, we tap into the rich vein of experience, expertise, and instinct that each MASSolutions team member possesses. This fusion of knowledge and data births innovative customer experience solutions and compelling stories that resonate on every level. It's about reaching out, connecting, engaging, altering perceptions, and shaping actions. As our flywheel spins, fueled by continuous insight and expertise, we create and refine solutions and stories that captivate and convert time and again.

This flywheel is a testament to the power of a holistic approach that marries marketing with every aspect of business strategy. You are encouraged to take that leap into developing your own flywheel just as Amazon did and as they inspired MASSolutions to do. Creating your custom flywheel brings you a living strategy that evolves with your business, market, and customers.

One of our superpowers is to gather insights by seeing what customers see and hearing what they think, which is explored in the next chapter.

14

SEE AND HEAR:
THE TWIN BEACONS OF CUSTOMER INSIGHT

To many, the work of mystery shoppers remains shrouded in mystery. Yet, if what your customers think and feel remains a mystery to you, it's time for a new approach.

"In the era of Yelp and TripAdvisor, when travelers can report anything at all to the Googling masses, trustworthy accounts are more important than ever to hoteliers," reports *Travel + Leisure* magazine about hotel mystery shoppers in an article titled "Confessions of A Hotel Mystery Shopper."[13]

Mystery shopping is a tried-and-tested method, but its full potential is often untapped in healthcare services. It's more than a covert evaluation. It's a direct line to seeing your service as your customers do.

However, at MASSolutions, we don't stop at the visual aspects. We listen intently to capture the voices of your customers. This dual approach—seeing through your customers' eyes and hearing what they say and feel—is pivotal for gaining complete customer insights and enhancing the stories we tell referral partners.

Observing through your customers' eyes via mystery shopping offers valuable insights into staff interactions and service delivery. Coupling this with the voice of customer interviews—asking open-ended questions and listening to the perceptions and opinions of those same customers—provides a more nuanced understanding of their experience.

Consider every touch point—the front desk, the tour guides, and healthcare providers. Mystery shopping allows you to learn about their performance, while voice-of-the-customer interviews enable you to hear the subtleties in customer feedback. Together, they highlight improvement areas and amplify your customers' why or reasons for buying from you.

Plus, you can leverage these customer insights to provide precise coaching for staff development and service enhancement.

The real game changer comes when combining these findings for referral source marketing in healthcare. Armed with concrete data and genuine insights, we can approach referral sources with compelling narratives, like the following example:

> *"Our latest mystery shopping and voice of the customer interviews reveal a clear picture. Our customers are thrilled when we do X, which we've been doing consistently. They're less enthusiastic about Y, and they've expressed a desire for Z. With this knowledge, we're reinforcing X, rethinking Y, and excitedly rolling out Z."*

Imagine how that resonates with a referral source accustomed to the same old pitches. Now, they have tangible reasons to confidently refer clients to you, knowing precisely what those clients will—and won't—experience.

So, let's leverage seeing through your customers' eyes by mystery shopping and hearing what your customers think via voice-of-the-customer interviews. It's a strategic way to understand what's working and what isn't, and it will drive the creation of our referral narratives. You can enhance the customer journey and craft a story that resonates across the board—from direct consumers to the professionals who recommend us.

Another tool that can be used to predict human behavior is explored in the next chapter.

15

USE BEHAVIORAL SCIENCE
TO MAXIMIZE B2E MARKETING

Think about it: it is hard to admit that we are not rational in our daily decisions.

"However, by admitting that we are biased, realizing that we should question our choices, and stepping outside of our comfort zone, we can open up our eyes to a whole new horizon," says author Ahmed AlAnsari.[14]

Behavioral science and analytics strip away this illusion by introducing data into our decision-making. Venturing out of our comfort zones and confronting our biases unlocks productivity and creativity. It's about probing beyond our assumptions to reveal the true forces shaping our behaviors and preferences.

This quest for authentic insight is why I'm always on the lookout for innovative tools and resources that question conventional wisdom and refine our strategic thinking.

A TOOL THAT IS A GAME CHANGER

One of my core beliefs is in the power of embracing challenges to find solutions that not only fulfill me personally
but also empower my team.

Whether coaching basketball, starting, growing, and
leading a company, or DJing at parties, bars, and weddings,
my aim has always been to inspire those around me to understand themselves, colleagues, and clients on a deeper level.

One tool that has been instrumental in helping me inspire
others on a deeper level is the Predictive Index or PI. This
scientifically validated assessment tool is a game changer
because it identifies what energizes individuals versus what
drains them.

The brilliance of the PI lies in its simplicity and accuracy.
It takes merely five minutes to complete, yet consistently
delivers insights that resonate deeply with those who take
it. The PI is astonishingly accurate, capturing the essence
of a person in a brief assessment. Skeptics are quickly con-
verted once they see how well it identifies their close asso-
ciates' traits, further proving its validity.

But how does this relate to healthcare and B2E marketing? Understanding the dynamics of what energizes
versus drains us is crucial in creating a harmonious and productive work environment. By integrating the PI, whether
across the entire organization or within specific teams like
marketing, we've observed remarkable improvements in
self-awareness and interpersonal relationships.

This tool allows individuals to recognize and adjust behaviors that might be taxing to others, fostering a culture of mutual respect and understanding. For instance, if one person's actions inadvertently drain another person's, we can facilitate a conversation to find a more harmonious approach to enhance team dynamics.

The impact of the PI extends beyond individual relationships. It plays a significant role in recruiting, retaining talent, and driving results by aligning employees' roles with their natural inclinations. This alignment boosts morale and elevates performance across the board, proving that the entire organization thrives when individuals understand themselves and their teammates better. It's a testament to the transformative power of B2E marketing, which focuses on empowering employees to bring out the best in one another.

PI can also be used to improve internal communication. Team leaders can craft their messaging to resonate more with each individual. We intuitively know to adjust our communication based on our audience and the setting. Bringing behavioral science into the equation reduces our inherent biases and clarifies potential blind spots.

Healthcare organizations ranging from large healthcare systems and insurers to senior living companies to home health and physical therapy providers have gleaned valuable insights that helped grow their businesses through stronger team cohesion, better referral source marketing, driving more leads, and greater organizational productivity.

You can gain more power to influence referral source behavior by interviewing multiple referral sources to find just the right stories. This approach is examined in the following chapter.

16

REFRAMING HOSPICE: A STORY OF CARING, LIVING, HEALING

Human brains are hardwired for stories. But how do you find the right referral stories?

The key is systematically gathering insights from your clearly defined target audiences, which drives the creative development of your overarching big idea and supporting storytelling pillars.

The next key step is to flesh out the anecdotes and analogies that tell a story about the big idea and each pillar. Your team will then repeatedly tell these multiple stories to each target market.

Your message begins to resonate, your target audiences connect with you, and your referrals increase. It's about growth marketing through creative storytelling driven by the insights you gather.

Here is an example of this strategy in action:

It highlights a hospice client and the profound insights we uncovered that reshaped their narrative. The common perception of hospice is as a last-resort service during the final days or weeks of a person's life. Yet, the reality is that hospice care can span months or even up to two years, a point not widely recognized.

Our mission was to refine our clients' messaging to resonate with patients and their families, enlighten referral sources, and energize employees. We embarked on an insightful journey, interviewing the hospice team, referral partners, and families to understand the essence of their service.

Through these conversations, we crafted a narrative encapsulating hospice care's multifaceted nature. It's not solely about end-of-life care or the caring part.

It's also about enabling precious moments of life, allowing patients and their families to cherish time together, fulfilling last wishes, and creating memories. This is hospice's "living" aspect—supporting patients to experience life fully in their remaining time.

Equally important was the "healing" aspect. We sought to guide families through their grieving process, offering a path to healing after their loved one's passing.

This holistic approach to care, life, and healing provided a new lens through which hospice could be viewed—an empathetic and life-affirming perspective.

For referral sources, this narrative was eye-opening. It encouraged them to consider hospice care earlier in the patient's journey, expanding their understanding of when and to whom hospice services could be beneficial. It wasn't just about the final days but about enhancing the quality of life for as long as possible.

This message also resonated deeply with current and potential employees, offering them a sense of pride and purpose in their work. It emphasized the dignity and compassion inherent in their roles and attracted those who shared this ethos to join the team.

But let's not overlook the power of storytelling in maximizing healthcare referrals. The stories we shape and share can profoundly influence referral sources, illustrating the broader impact of hospice care on patients and families.

Take, for example, the touching story of a grandfather who, under our hospice's care, attended a Pittsburgh Pirates game with his grandson. It was more than just an outing; it was a fulfillment of a lifelong dream, a day imbued with love, captured in candid snapshots and videos that would become a cherished memory for the family.

In those moments at PNC Park, our narrative of living, not just existing, came to life. It was a testament to the "living" component of hospice care, a story that echoed the essence of our message—care, life, and healing intertwined.

Every hospice and healthcare organization has such success stories; these narratives must be told with conviction and frequency. They underscore the transformative power of hospice care and its ability to touch lives profoundly. It's not just about the care provided; it's about fostering life and guiding the journey toward healing.

Let me close this book by looking ahead at the forces on the horizon you should consider as you build your referral marketing program.

17

INTO THE FUTURE

As we stand on the cusp of a new era in healthcare services marketing, the horizon is filled with transformative trends that will redefine how we drive referrals and engage with our customers and employees. Artificial intelligence (AI), the talent wars, generational marketing, the evolution of social media, and healthcare referral gatekeepers are among the vanguards of this change.

ARTIFICIAL INTELLIGENCE: KEEPING IT REAL

Frankly, I am loathe to write about AI in a book because the changes are coming so rapidly.

AI's role in marketing isn't to replace human creativity but to enhance it. Take, for example, a client who joked about being "ChatGPT'd" due to the obvious AI tone of a consultant's emails. It shows that AI needs a human touch to be truly effective.

That said, I believe AI can help speed up the process

for producing basic, lower-level content and messaging. This will affect the marketing field to some degree because tools like ChatGPT, Jasper, and many new ones coming out regularly can mimic the work of marginal content creators.

Here's how we employ the 80/20 principle in our three-step AI strategy at MASSolutions:

1. *The primer:* Begin with a one-time comprehensive setup of your AI tool. Inform it about your voice, values, and unique elements. It's critical to get this foundation right and remember that it's not set in stone—adjust as you grow and as things change.

2. *The stream of consciousness:* Next, for any specific task, channel your raw thoughts directly into the AI tool, moving your ideas into electronic form quickly. This process, combined with the primer from step one, swiftly takes your concept from inception to an 80 percent complete draft, leveraging the 80/20 rule for maximum efficiency.

3. *The polish:* The last 20 percent is where you transform your initial draft into a polished piece that's 100 percent yours and reflects your voice, ideas, and human touch. Your insights, tone, and personal flair elevate the content from generic to genuinely yours.

This systematic approach melds AI's rapid capabilities with your authentic voice. It embodies the 80/20 rule, optimizing time and retaining the personal touch crucial to outstanding marketing.

B2E MARKETING: THE TALENT MAGNET

B2E marketing is not just the future; it's the now. It goes beyond filling roles; it's about aligning with the *whys* of your potential and current employees. Understanding their motivations, segmenting accordingly, and crafting resonating messages leads to a robust recruiting and retention strategy. When infused with systematic insights and data-driven storytelling, this approach doesn't just fill vacancies—it enhances productivity and enriches company culture. B2E Marketing drives talent acquisition, employee retention, and creation of your culture story, which are three crucial areas for any company.

B2E MARKETING: CRAFTING THE EMPLOYEE NARRATIVE

In B2E marketing, we advocate a tectonic shift toward companies recognizing employees as their first customers. Engaging current and prospective employees through targeted storytelling humanizes the brand and fosters loyalty and advocacy.

We can create environments where every team member feels integral to the mission by systematically gathering insights from and about current and prospective employees and then developing and articulating a company narrative that resonates with their personal and professional aspirations.

This strategy has repeatedly proven its mettle, translating into tangible benefits such as reduced turnover rates, heightened employee satisfaction, and a discernible uptick in productivity. The stories we craft are not merely for external consumption; they are the bedrock of our internal ethos.

SOCIAL MEDIA: THE DISCIPLINE OF FOCUS

Social media's challenge lies in its distractibility. The inundation of notifications can derail productivity, making discipline in consumption crucial. As much as we might claim proficiency in multitasking, science tells us it's a myth. Focused, uninterrupted work, like productive mornings, leads to significant achievements. For social media to serve us rather than govern us, we must wield it with intentional restraint.

Social media's double-edged sword presents a unique challenge in the digital age. On one hand, it's a potent tool for storytelling and customer engagement. Conversely, it's a vortex of distraction that can dilute focus and productivity.

We advocate for a disciplined approach to social media consumption to harness its power without falling prey to its pitfalls. By scheduling dedicated "social sprints," we can engage with our audience and then retreat to deep work, ensuring that the constant pings of connectivity do not fragment our creative energies. This mindful approach to social media is critical in maintaining a balance between staying connected and preserving the cognitive space necessary for innovation.

GENERATIONAL WISDOM: BEYOND STEREOTYPES

While generational studies offer valuable frameworks for marketing strategies, they are not absolutes. Each generation contains individuals who defy age-based expectations. A nuanced approach that appreciates this diversity within generational cohorts will yield more personalized and effective marketing strategies.

By embracing a plan that recognizes each generational group's unique preferences and behaviors, we unlock the potential for highly personalized marketing. This nuanced understanding allows us to craft messages that resonate on a deeper level, fostering a connection that transcends generational boundaries.

REFERRAL SOURCE GATEKEEPERS: THE UNSEEN INFLUENCERS

Healthcare gatekeepers often hold the keys to referral flow in healthcare marketing. Whether it's the office manager for a group of physicians or the case manager at a hospital, tailoring your message to these pivotal roles is as important as addressing the healthcare professionals themselves. A nuanced approach that adapts the channel and message to the gatekeeper's perspective can unlock new referral opportunities.

The strategic pivot here involves crafting dual narratives that appeal to healthcare providers' clinical and professional sensibilities and another that resonates with gatekeepers' operational and administrative priorities. By differentiating the messaging to cater to these distinct perspectives, we unlock new referral streams and deepen our engagement with healthcare gatekeepers. This dual narrative approach is a testament to our commitment to understanding and addressing the nuanced needs of every stakeholder in the healthcare journey.

MY PARTING WISHES FOR YOU

In conclusion, the future of healthcare marketing is an intricate tapestry woven from AI, talent strategy, social media discipline, generational insights, and an understanding of referral dynamics. It's a future where no bullsh!t marketing principles—segmentation, insight gathering, and science-backed storytelling—remain at the core, ensuring that our strategies are as human as they are data-driven.

The future is bright, and as we navigate these changes, we'll continue to share stories, build connections, and drive referrals in innovative, empathetic, and, above all, effective ways.

APPENDICES

ACKNOWLEDGMENTS

The genesis of this book lies in the values my parents instilled in me: determination, drive, and an insatiable hunger to learn. They gave me the ability to turn complexity into simplicity and to communicate, educate, and motivate others about these clear-cut solutions. To this day, they continue to inspire me with their vitality, their humor, and their unwavering love.

Thank you to my brother, a brilliant writer who provided support and unconditional belief in my vision.

A thank you also to my sons, Alec, Brevin, and Carter, who each uniquely bolstered this book and my resolve. Alec, your encouragement fueled my confidence during moments of doubt. Brevin, your perspective was a beacon through my frustrations, keeping me aligned with our goals. Carter, your ideas and role reversal, coaching me when I most needed it, were indispensable.

Henry DeVries, you asked the right questions and listened intently, making sure we stayed true to the no bullsh!t mantra. Your editorial acumen brought clarity and impact to these pages.

My MASSolutions team has been instrumental every step of the way. Your support, feedback, and encouragement not only enriched this book but also fortified our daily mission to deliver exceptional marketing and storytelling.

Our clients, who have entrusted us with their marketing and branding, continuously inspire us to harness our unique abilities to find strategic marketing solutions and tell stories that resonate and persuade.

I am also immensely grateful to the leaders who have been pivotal in my career—David Smith, John Dame, George Hartnett, Tony Lombardi, and John Paul. Each of you instilled lessons that have profoundly shaped my professional journey.

Thank you to Chuck Gounaris for being a trusted advisor and sounding board over the years.

And to the many friends, family members, and business colleagues whose names are too numerous to list but are not forgotten, your contributions to my life and this book are deeply appreciated. Your collective wisdom, encouragement, and support have left indelible marks on these pages and my heart.

Thank you all for being part of this story.

ABOUT THE AUTHOR

Dave Mastovich is the dynamic and bold CEO and Founder of MASSolutions, a strategic marketing consultancy known for driving growth through innovative marketing solutions and creative storytelling.

An accomplished author and prolific content creator as the No Bullsh!t Marketer, Dave's insights have been featured in over 200 media outlets. His blog and podcast, with over 500 episodes, are go-to resources for leaders seeking to leverage the power of strategic marketing and creative storytelling without the fluff. His first book, *Get Where You Want to Go Through Marketing, Selling, and Storytelling,* continues to help people achieve their growth goals.

Dave focuses on cognitive science and 80/20 analysis to drive the creative art. His trademarked approach includes systematic insights gathering, precise target market analysis, and developing marketing solutions that enhance the customer experience. Under his marketing leadership and strategies, hundreds of companies have experienced remarkable growth, boosted employee engagement, enhanced brand awareness, and elevated enterprise value.

His deep understanding of pop culture trends makes him a sought-after speaker. He infuses these trends into his challenging and pro-growth narratives, creating compelling stories that resonate with diverse audiences.

Dave's love for basketball spans decades of playing and coaching. He has had the joy of coaching all three of his sons and sharing his knowledge and passion for the game. He still wants the ball in his hands in the final seconds.

He also enjoys listening to music, going to concerts, walking outdoors every day, working out, and embracing new experiences, even cold plunging.

Dave and his family live in the suburbs of Pittsburgh, Pennsylvania. He operates between MASSolutions's offices in Pittsburgh and Long Beach, California. His commitment to marketing excellence and memorable storytelling continues to inspire businesses to achieve their full potential.

For speaking engagements or consulting inquiries, please contact Dave at

dave@massolutions.biz

https://www.linkedin.com/in/davidmmastovich/

https://massolutions.biz/

ENDNOTES

1 Philip Kotler, *The Principles of Marketing* (Upper Saddle River, NJ: Prentice Hall, 1983).

2 Anwesha Nag, "Everybody Has a Plan Until They Get Punched in the Mouth. How Did the Famous Mike Tyson Quote Originate?" Sportskeeda, modified January 5, 2021, https://www.sportskeeda.com/mma/news-everybody-plan-get-punched-mouth-how-famous-mike-tyson-quote-originate.

3 Fred Ebband and John Kander, "Theme from *New York, New York*," New York, 1977, reprised by Frank Sinatra.

4 Cameron Crowe, dir., *Jerry Maguire*, Culver City, CA: Tri-Star Pictures, 1996.

5 Henry DeVries, *Persuade with a Story* (Oceanside, CA: Indie Books International, 2016).

6 Francis Ford Coppola, dir., *The Godfather*, Hollywood, CA: Paramount Pictures, 1972.

7 "Notes to Measurement in Science," Stanford Encyclopedia of Philosophy, accessed May 16, 2024, https://plato.stanford.edu/entries/measurement-science/notes.html.

8 Lloyd Corder, *The Snapshot Survey: Quick, Affordable Marketing Research for Every Organization* (London: Kaplan Publishing, 2006).

9 Ron Howard, dir., *Apollo 13*, Hollywood, CA: Universal Studios, 1995, https://spacecenter.org/apollo-13-infographic-how-did-they-make-that-co2-scrubber/.

10 Simon Sinek, *Start with Why: How Great Leaders Inspire Everyone to Take Action* (New York: Portfolio, 2009).

11 Simon Sinek, "Start with Why: How Great Leaders Inspire Action," TEDxPugetSound, 2009, video, 18:01, https://www.youtube.com/watch?v=u4ZoJKF_VuA.

12 Jim Collins, *Good to Great* (New York: Harper Publishers, 2001).

13 Kathryn O'Shea-Evans, "Confessions of a Hotel Mystery Shopper," *Travel + Leisure*, June 20, 2012, https://www.travelandleisure.com/hotels-resorts/hotel-reviews/confessions-of-a-hotel-mystery-shopper.

14 Ahmed AlAnsari and Hamza AlGhatam, *The Brand Dependence Model: Identify & Mitigate Your Danger Blocks* (self-pub., 2002).

www.ingramcontent.com/pod-product-compliance
Lightning Source LLC
Chambersburg PA
CBHW031948190326
41519CB00007B/708